Dear Parents and Educators,

Welcome to Penguin Young Readers! As parents and educators, you know that each child develops at his or her own pace—in terms of speech, critical thinking, and, of course, reading. Penguin Young Readers recognizes this fact. As a result, each Penguin Young Readers book is assigned a traditional easy-to-read level (1–4) as well as a Guided Reading Level (A–P). Both of these systems will help you choose the right book for your child. Please refer to the back of each book for specific leveling information. Penguin Young Readers features esteemed authors and illustrators, stories about favorite characters, fascinating nonfiction, and more!

Snail-Snaily-Snails

LEVEL 2

GUIDED READING LEVEL **I**

This book is perfect for a **Progressing Reader** who:
- can figure out unknown words by using picture and context clues;
- can recognize beginning, middle, and ending sounds;
- can make and confirm predictions about what will happen in the text; and
- can distinguish between fiction and nonfiction.

Here are some **activities** you can do during and after reading this book:
- Nonfiction: Nonfiction books deal with facts and events that are real. Talk about the elements of nonfiction. On a separate sheet of paper, write down what you learned about snails.
- Compare/Contrast: In this book, we learn that there is more than one kind of snail. How are garden snails different from pond snails? How are they similar?

Remember, sharing the love of reading with a child is the best gift you can give!

—Sarah Fabiny, Editorial Director
  Penguin Young Readers program

*Penguin Young Readers are leveled by independent reviewers applying the standards developed by Irene Fountas and Gay Su Pinnell in *Matching Books to Readers: Using Leveled Books in Guided Reading*, Heinemann, 1999.

For Lauren, who used to pick up snails
on the way to school—BB

PENGUIN YOUNG READERS
An Imprint of Penguin Random House LLC

Photo credits: cover: Leo Malsam/iStock/Thinkstock; page 3: Rclassenlayouts/iStock/Thinkstock;
page 4: Napat_Polchoke/iStock/Thinkstock; page 5: Alex Popov/Hemera/Thinkstock; page 6: (top)
Rclassenlayouts/iStock/Thinkstock, (middle) Hydromet/iStock/Thinkstock, (bottom)
BSANI/iStock/Thinkstock; page 7: (top) GlobalP/iStock/Thinkstock, (middle)
Leoshoot/iStock/Thinkstock, (bottom, left and right) Rclassenlayouts/iStock/Thinkstock; page 8:
(top) Frans Rombout/iStock/Thinkstock, (bottom) IvanMikhaylov/iStock/Thinkstock; page 9:
Zoonar RF/Zoonar/Thinkstock; page 10: Ingram Publishing/Thinkstock; page 11: (top)
Grahamhaynes/iStock/Thinkstock, (middle) Ananaline/iStock/Thinkstock, (bottom)
Khajornkiat/iStock/Thinkstock; page 12: Scubaluna//iStock/Thinkstock; page 13:
Dogwin/iStock/Thinkstock; page 14: (top) Jupiterimages/Photos.com/Thinkstock, (bottom)
MirceaX/iStock/Thinkstock; page 15: Ingrid Adegaard/iStock/Thinkstock; page 16:
DEMIURGE_100/iStock/Thinkstock; page 17: Defun/iStock/Thinkstock; page 18:
GlobalP/iStock/Thinkstock; page 19: ImageBROKER/Superstock; page 20:
Scubaluna/iStock/Thinkstock; page 21: Rex/Wikimedia Commons; page 22:
Oliver Meadows/iStock/Thinkstock; page 23: 4028mdk09/Wikimedia Commons (CC BY-SA 3.0)
(background removed); page 24: Oxford Scientist/Photodisc/Getty Images; page 25:
Donald Burgess/Ardea.com/Pantheon/Pa/Superstock; page 26:
David Fleetham/Visuals Unlimited/Getty Images; page 27: B. Páll-Gergely and N. Szpisjak (CC BY 4.0);
page 28: (top left) GlobalP/iStock/Thinkstock, (top right) Adogslifephoto/iStock/Thinkstock, (bottom)
Tonivaver/iStock/Thinkstock; page 29: (top left) GlobalP/iStock/Thinkstock, (top right)
PhotoObjects.net/Thinkstock, (bottom left) UncleScrooge/iStock/Thinkstock, (bottom right)
Vasyl Helevachuk/iStock/Thinkstock; pages 30–31: Westend61/Getty Images; page 32:
Janie Airey/DigitalVision/Getty Images.

Library of Congress Cataloging-in-Publication Data is available.

ISBN 9780451534392 (pbk)   10 9 8 7 6 5 4 3 2 1
ISBN 9780451534408 (hc)   10 9 8 7 6 5 4 3 2 1

PENGUIN YOUNG READERS

LEVEL **2**

PROGRESSING READER

snail-snaily-snails

by Bonnie Bader

Penguin Young Readers
An Imprint of Penguin Random House

Snail.

Snaily.

Snails!

Snails have soft bodies.

They are like oysters and clams.

A snail's body is soft
and wet and slimy.

A snail's shell

keeps its body safe.

A snail can hide in its shell.

Some shells are tall.

Some shells are flat.

Most snail shells are smooth.

But some are hairy!

Some snails live in gardens.

A snail creeps across the garden.

It leaves a trail of slime.

The slime helps it

hang on to plants.

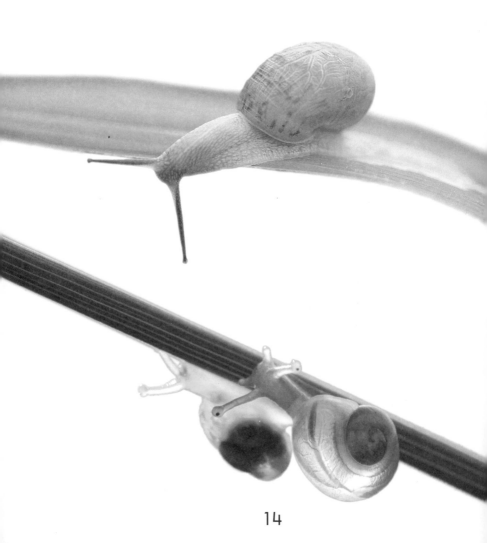

Snails eat plants.

Many people do not like

snails in their gardens.

A snail uses its tentacles

to feel around.

Garden snails have

four tentacles.

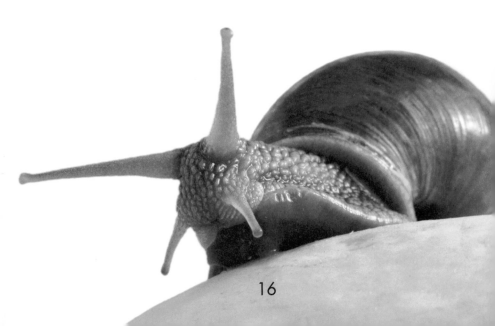

How does a snail see?

A garden snail has eyes

on the tips of its long tentacles.

Snails also live in ponds.

Pond snails are dark brown.

Some pond snails have gills,
like fish.

Gills help snails breathe
under the water.

Other pond snails have
a kind of lung.
They float to the top of the water
to breathe.

A pond snail has two tentacles.

It has eyes at the base

of its tentacles.

Garden snails do not like the sun.

Garden snails like the rain.

Garden snails like the night.

Dry weather is not good

for a garden snail.

So it goes into its shell

and closes up the opening.

A garden snail lays its eggs

deep in the dirt.

One snail can lay up to 85 eggs.

As soon as the baby snails hatch,

they look for food.

The babies can eat their own

eggshells or other eggs.

The largest snail in the world can grow to 18 inches long.

This snail lives in the ocean.

It can even eat starfish!

The smallest snail is very tiny.

Ten of these tiny snails could

fit in the eye of a needle

at the same time!

Watch out, little snails!

Beetles, snakes, toads, turtles,

chickens, ducks, and geese

like to eat all kinds of snails.

You can catch snails

and put them in a clear jar.

Be sure the jar is open or

has some small holes.

Put some leaves in the jar.

Watch the snails move slowly.

Munch, crunch,

snail, snaily, snail.